SCOTLAND IN OLD PHOTOGRAPHS

ELGIN PEOPLE

JENNY MAIN

SUTTON PUBLISHING LIMITED

Sutton Publishing Limited
Phoenix Mill · Thrupp · Stroud
Gloucestershire · GL5 2BU

First published 1998

Copyright © Jenny Main, 1998

British Library Cataloguing in Publication Data
A catalogue record for this book is available from the
British Library.

ISBN 0-7509-1693-1

Typeset in 10/12 Perpetua.
Typesetting and origination by
Sutton Publishing Limited.
Printed in Great Britain by
Ebenezer Baylis, Worcester.

CONTENTS

Lossie Wynd, between the wars. The garage became Hughes the chemist. Anderson & England was here until the 1960s.

INTRODUCTION

This is certainly not a definitive collection of Elgin people, for that would be impossible to achieve within a small book. It is simply a random selection, giving a brief flavour of different days when there was less concern with social life, but more community involvement. Superficialities change, but the basics of human nature do not. Old stories illustrate our diversity, as well as the things we have, and always have had, in common.

'My father used to have to walk about three miles to school every day, from Longmorn to New Elgin, from the time he was five years old.'

'There were thirteen of us to feed and I mind we used to take a pillowcase to the baker's to get it filled with loaf ends – or to the butcher's to get bones for boiling for broth.'

'As bairns we would take a pram to the gas works and collect cinders for our fire, and we would often go to the woods to collect cones for kindling.'

'. . . then there was the sweetie shop at the bottom of Moss Street, with sugar mice and home-made toffee, and Mrs Officer who lived until she was over 100.'

Elgin has always had its fair share of fondly remembered characters and 'worthies'. In the recent past folk still recall 'Chocolate Leggies' with the thick glasses, who collected waste paper in a barrow – to the delight of the mischievous loons who would tip it up; 'Tabby Hector', Hector Lindsay, who played just a couple of tunes on his melodeon; 'Coffee' Homack, who reputedly had served in the Kenyan police, and swam daily in the Lossie, diving in from a tree near the Bow Brig. There were the Shoggies – called Omo and Daz in reference to their cleanliness. Then there was Big Joanne McCulloch who needed several hefty 'polis' to escort her to the station. Once installed and recovered from her excesses, she would clean the cells spotless and wash the blankets thoroughly, grumbling, with some justification, that this was the only reason she was 'lifted' so frequently! The renowned 'Forty Pockets' wore layer upon layer of coats and is reputed to have walked the length of the entire Scottish railways. 'Thummacks' was born with two thumbs on one hand and sold collar studs and laces. 'The Moley' John McDonald, molecatcher and puppeteer, used to proclaim proudly that he had 'played to the crowned heads of Europe, all over the world – and many other places beside.'

Nostalgia thrives in a close community like Elgin where if you 'skelp ae lug they a' dirl'. It seems inevitable that every generation believes the days of their youth were 'the good old days' and any changes from then rarely seem to be for the better. Innovations such as electricity and the motor car, so often taken for granted, altered lives dramatically. In seventy years' time the babies of today will doubtless recall the future decades with fondness, while today's teenagers will eventually bemoan the forthcoming pace of life and decline in 'standards'.

The clearest sight is hindsight and it is only too easy to judge from the safety of distance. None of us knows how well we may have coped within the limitations of past conditions and we can only admire the effort made by so many to improve their environment, their town and their community. To an older generation it is not always immediately obvious why the youngsters of today behave so apparently irrationally. To a new generation it is not apparent why things were once done so differently. The 'good old days' around the turn of the century were also days of unimaginable poverty. People lost life and limb because of lack of the health facilities we now take for granted. Many were unable to afford a doctor and consequently resorted to dangerous folk remedies with often tragic results. Many women died in childbirth and many men were killed in accidents or in war, which explains the subsequent large families of half-brothers and sisters. During three months in 1896, 48 out of 318 Elgin births were illegitimate.

Many workers were obliged to struggle in miserable and dangerous conditions. Living in tied houses, they stood to lose home as well as employment and good references if they made any complaints. On some of the estates the employees were obliged to attend the local church every Sunday or risk their livelihood. Domestic servants performing the more menial household tasks could be instantly dismissed if found offending their employers with their presence in the wrong part of the house after 8 a.m. One local estate had a special 'Low Walk' constructed so that the sight of common folk going about their business did not impinge on the view and sensibilities of the gentry.

It wasn't all repression and depression. There were many opportunities for fun and laughter and many employers were benevolent and paternal towards their staff, taking responsibility for the welfare of their workers and families. Once settled into a suitable situation people could normally expect to have a job for life.

This century has seen incredible changes in people's lives. The most dramatic impact has been owing to the effect of two devastating world wars. Many from the Elgin area willingly volunteered to fight for their country. Apart from enormous loss of the lives of those directly involved in the fighting, the families and friends left at home had their world irrevocably altered. War didn't just kill, it maimed and disabled physically and mentally. The loss to the community of so many people, the loss of so much potential, cannot be calculated, and the ruin to so many future hopes should never be underestimated.

Thanks to the generosity of people who have been willing to share their memories and photographs, it is possible to glimpse how the pattern of the present has been woven from the threads of the past. Memories are precious, and it is a privilege to be able to share them.

Jenny Main

CHAPTER 1

WORTHIES & WORKERS

The old worthies of Elgin were erratic, eccentric characters whose antics enlivened the lives of their neighbours. Before the provisions of the welfare state many had to struggle to survive, and some did manage to obtain occasional simple work. Those burdened with what we now recognize as psychological and psychiatric problems often ended up in the Poor House or the Asylum. Others with perseverance endeared themselves to benefactors and survived tolerably well until obliged to apply for Poor Relief. Meanwhile, before the advent of labour-saving machinery and the protection of unions, large squads of men undertook the varied and heavy labour-intensive work necessary in the thriving community.

James 'Dog' Cormie, a renowned storyteller. He lived in a hovel in the east end of Elgin with sixteen dogs, a badger, a monkey, an old grey mare called Kate, a wife and two 'coorse quines'. A groom at Gordon Castle in his youth, he was always welcomed there by the 5th Duke. One evening in 1854, returning home early, he was enraged to discover a young stable-lad being 'entertained'. 'Dog' Cormie chased him down the street, blasting both barrels of his fowling piece at the offender's rear. Thanks to his friends, including the Duke of Gordon, 'Dog' was saved from a possible hanging. He was buried in a pauper's grave in 1866.

John 'Pickie' Gow, by trade a tanner, preferred the thrill of poaching and was well known to local lairds and gamekeepers. He was buried in the precincts of the cathedral in 1922 and it is said his gravestone was laid flat on the ground instead of upright in order to make sure that he did not return to torment them with his poaching again!

Peter Laing died in 1890 aged 103 after an estimated 70,000 plates of porridge during that time! He advised, 'Tak as few dainties as ye can, plenty o' porridge and brose, tak plenty fresh air and dinna birsle yer shins ower mickle at the fire!' A farm servant at Dallas, he recalled supping porridge at three in the morning 'wi' plenty barley bread tae haud it doon'. Porridge was made with milk in summer, with the odd treat of 'a plate o' haddocks and sauce'. 'Diner wi' biled sowens and bread and supper a bowl o' brose, or kail porridge, perhaps.'

James McDonald, 'The Dummy'. Research has yielded little about this character; from his nickname he was presumably deaf and dumb. It is an interesting illustration of a cobbler at work when such a trade was in great demand for repairing leather soles and 'tackety' boots. The clay pipe was once a common object before the habit was refined by the tobacco companies with their more convenient and expensive cigarettes.

William Watson, 'Bowsie'. Known as the great chieftain of the Elgin characters of his day, Bowsie was adept at handling horses. At one time he had driven the 'four in hand' from Elgin to Inverness and often boasted of his many adventures whenever he was suitably refreshed. His name is presumed to be a corruption of 'boozie'. Although he did have a weakness for drink, his swift wit and clever sallies earned enough gratuities to keep him happy.

James 'Punchie' Grant, born 1794, the youngest of a family of twenty-four. His father, who had a barber's shop, was the best wig-maker in the county. 'Punchie', an excellent shoemaker, entertained with singing and poetry recitals and was skilled with rod and spear in the days when salmon were plentiful. He reputedly caught a basketful of pike using a piece of red flannel for bait. He would give away cartloads of free fish and was much mourned when he died, aged eighty. He is buried in the old graveyard at Kirkhill where his many friends contributed towards the headstone.

John Shanks, shoemaker (1758–1841). Living opposite the Muckle Cross, he was appointed keeper of the cathedral in 1824. In seventeen years he removed nearly 3,000 barrowfuls of rubble from the site which had been neglected for more than 120 years. His work revealed much of the original cathedral, inspiring others to complete the task. He is standing here in front of a gravestone inscribed, 'This world is a cite full of streets & death is the mercat that all men meets. If lyfe were a thing that monie could buy te poor could not live & te rich would not die.'

'Cutler' Jamie Murdoch. Cutler Jamie was a taciturn local poet. His verses were influenced by his own hard experiences of life, being melancholy and generally pessimistic, and appeared in the poet's corner of the local paper, the *Courant*.

Andy and his dog Bobbie. Andrew Mackenzie, innocent and harmless, known as 'feel Andy', was slightly built and had a quick springy walk and run. He would catch bullfinches in the Oakwood with the aid of bird-lime or a trap cage. His collection of pigeons had free run of his house and were allowed outside for exercise. He would often sit on top of his rickety stair with his poulter pigeons and white fantails fluttering around him. Following the death of his parents he was looked after in Elgin's mental institution, where he died at the age of forty-six.

'Yeukie Hugh'. Quiet and morose, Hugh Brown occasionally drove cattle to the slaughterhouse, or the Market Green. His name derived from his habit of 'hodgin' his shoulders every few minutes, as if tormented by an uncontrollable itch. His antique straw hat, worn in summer, had cost him one penny at a sale. He had a well-seasoned clay 'cutty' with a 'reddin pin', chained to the stalk, stowed in his waistcoat pocket. He was obsessed with watches and his waistcoat displayed an array of metal, leather, hair and twine 'alberts'. He took great pride in telling the time by consulting a verge, lever or Geneva.

'Johnny Frostie', William Russell (1779–1863).
He was born at Cowfords Farm near
Mosstodloch, the youngest of a family of twelve.
Graduating with honours from Aberdeen
University, he took his final degree as a minister,
then wandered around America working as an
office clerk. He never bought shoes after
returning home in 1810, but would wander up to
fifty miles a day, having a daily dip in a river
whatever the weather. Witty and knowledgeable,
welcome in many parlours, he would play classical
and Scottish airs on his fiddle. He was buried in
the old graveyard at Dipple.

John Cruickshank Bannochie (1814–88),
upholsterer and well-known public heckler. He
enlivened many public meetings with his fierce
tirades against the iniquities and bungling of the
councillors. The MP for Elgin Burgh, Mr Grant
Duff, was a renowned, if monotonous, speaker
on subjects ranging from China to Peru and,
consequently, known as 'the member for the
universe'. Unimpressed, John Bannochie would
fiercely flourish his roll of memoranda and
questions, demanding to know why Mr Grant
had voted as he had done on various issues. He
drowned at the public baths at the age of
seventy-four.

A large cast-iron flywheel, ready for action. The story behind this picture has been lost, but because of its size, it is unlikely that the flywheel has just been newly cast at the Newmill factory. It is more probable that the wheel is about to be installed in a factory, such as one of the woollen mills. No doubt someone will have the answer! Meanwhile we can appreciate the effort in making and installing such a massive object and imagine the enormous size of machine for which it would be required.

A smiddy at Crook of Alves in the early 1930s. Standing by the great cartwheel, left to right, are Hamie Cattenach, Peter Vass, Donald Cattenach with the dog and Sandy Taylor. There were several smiddys in the small village of Alves at the turn of the century, all kept busy with the demands from local farms and estates, horses and horse-drawn vehicles. At the end of the century very few men possess the skills required of the old smiths.

Group of forestry workers in Monaughty, Pluscarden, 1930s. 'I used to work with some of those lads in 1925. It was my first job when I left school at 3s a day. I cycled from Westerton Lodge at 7 a.m. to join Mr Robbie's squad at Monaughty and if it was wet in the morning we got no pay. I can mind when J. Robbie went to Africa . . . he used to live with Mrs Sim in Pluscarden.'

Workers at Cardow Distillery, 1902. The whisky distilleries have played a vital role in the development of Moray. Cardow, now Cardhu, distillery, Aberlour, was established in 1824, supplied with water from the Mannoch Hill and the Lyne Burn, and now receives over 16,000 visitors a year. This picture shows some of the past employees. Jimmy Gordon, the brewer, sits in the centre, with his small son Joe between his feet. Joe was killed in the First World War. Third from the left is the distillery's Customs & Excise officer, wearing a hard hat.

In the garden of Pitgaveny, 1890s. The greenhouse was demolished in 1896, which helps date the photograph. In the chair sits Captain James Brander Dunbar Brander surrounded by some of the staff. In the bowler hat is Stiff, the coachman; Jessie the cook is third from the right; 'Black' Bob Geddes is on the extreme right. Behind the chair, in his kilt, is the Captain's son, James Brander Dunbar, 'The Lairdie'. A mourning band is visible on his right arm, and on close inspection it can be seen that his father is also wearing one.

The building of Cromdale Bridge, 1921. George Geddes used a squad of men from Newton Quarry to build the new bridge. Standing on the left of the picture is George Geddes (1875–1937) and in the front row with the lads is his son George (1903–97).

Cromdale Bridge under construction, 1921. Originally there was a ferry here, then two bridges, which were each swept away. The locals started a collection to build a new bridge and Moray County Council and the Ministry of Transport helped towards the cost, which was £2,000. The contractor, George Geddes, can be seen standing in the middle of the bridge, supervising construction.

Apprentice painters, 1870s. On the left is A. McCulloch, and on the right William Fordyce. William Fordyce, who was born in 1856, eventually became a master painter. From 1896 he had his own business at 69 High Street, Elgin, and had the reputation of being one of the best grainers and signwriters in the north. He was a strong advocate of the temperance society and a regular member of Elgin High Church. He died in 1940 and his business was taken over by his foreman – the firm was known by then as Fordyce & Gentleman.

Workmen at the firm of John Kintrae, house painter. On the right is William Fordyce, who was foreman there. He then went to Forres and set up his own business there from 1889 until 1896, before moving to Elgin as painter and signwriter. He was an uncle of John Brodie, who eventually became Provost of Elgin. While William did the painting from a makeshift sling contraption (which was cheaper than scaffolding) John did the plasterwork of the old Elgin Town Hall.

Tile works at Windyridge in the late 1930s. This tile and brickworks was just off the Elgin–Lossiemouth road and the old clay pit is now a pond. The hatless man in the back row was Stewart Kelman, one of the many blacksmiths of the time.

Christie's Nurseries, Fochabers, c. 1920. Who then could have envisaged the changes to come in horticulture? With the increased popularity of gardening and the variety of accessories now available, Christie's Nurseries have expanded and changed, with a large shop meeting the needs of today's leisure gardeners.

Robert Main, trawler fisherman, *c.* 1920. Much of Moray's wealth came from the sea, Elgin's growth owing a great deal to the fishing industry. Fishermen would set off to sea for months at a time, decks laden down with sufficient coal to take them into the deadly North Sea waters. Finding a dry place on board was almost impossible. Comforts were few and dangers many. Most fishermen refused to learn to swim, believing that if they fell overboard death would then come more quickly and mercifully. Unsurprisingly, Robert did not wish his sons to follow him to sea.

Hydro Board worker, 1960s, and a far cry from the dangers of the seas where his grandfather Robert earned a living. George Main faced different but nonetheless deadly dangers which were unimaginable in his grandfather's day. With his colleagues he was called out on many a stormy night to repair damage to the lines and restore electrical power to the consumers.

CHAPTER 2

CITY BUSTLE

Work and work requirements have altered over the years, as have attitudes. With the advent of easily accessible transport and communications, the pace of life has also changed immensely. Different yardsticks have to be used, which makes true comparisons between the old and the new ways impossible. All that can be agreed upon is that things were very different then for everybody.

Elgin Trades Incorporation outside the Old Town Hall. This picture is undated, but a top hat and the cigarette in evidence on the front row suggest that it was taken just before the First World War. Craft guilds were first mentioned in Scotland in about 1151 when King David I allowed burgesses to associate in defence of their rights of free trade within the burgh. In the thirteenth century the Trades of Perth, Aberdeen, Stirling, Elgin, Berwick and Dundee were entitled to form themselves into Corporations. Every craft, with its own patron saint, separate altar and priest, had its place within St Giles' Church. Following the sixteenth-century Reformation, the Hammermen, Glovers, Tailors, Shoemakers, Weavers and Squarewrights formed themselves into a Convenery to protect their privileges. Their powerful influence on local industry was only curtailed by the Reform Act of 1832.

William Naughty, a rope spinner, who lived in the Star Inn Close. He died in 1892, aged forty-six, of injuries sustained in a fire at the Star Hotel. The craft of rope-making is an ancient one. Hemp was used in Europe from 200 BC and remained in use until the nineteenth century when it was replaced by Manila hemp, an unrelated plant from the Philippines. This in turn was replaced in the 1950s by synthetic materials. Rope factories produced essential ropes for the fishing, agriculture, commercial and construction industries. This photograph gives an interesting insight into living accommodation of the time.

Mrs Holmes, born in 1907, making nets at the net factory of Low & Son. She was employed there for forty-five years and must have had a prodigious output of this essential product. The factory was sited on Wards Road and the building is still in existence.

Clerks of Grigor & Young, solicitors, 1871. This picture illustrates one of the dramatic ways in which society has changed. Before the dawn of the modern typewriter in 1873, and the two world wars of the twentieth century, the office workers were almost entirely men.

Staff of Grigor & Young enjoying an evening out in the Gordon Arms Hotel, 1950s. Back row, left to right: Marion Skiff, Libby Grigor, Primmy Forbes, Susan Hay, Nancy Dawson. Second row: Anne Smith, Marion Sinclair, Audrey Allan, Mary Smart, Dorothy Gow, Eleanor Gilhooley. Third row: Helen Johnstone, Margaret Grigor, Mary Farquhar, Winnie Hardy, Betty Calder, Daphne Brodie. Front row: Bill ?, W.G. Young, W.C. Knox, A.F. Black, A.M. Horne.

A maid at the turn of the century. Seated on the front steps of Pitgaveny House with four dogs, this unnamed maid in her lace pin-tucked apron was lucky to have a 'place' in service, although the hours could be long and the work arduous in some houses.

Nine young ladies at the turn of the century. There is no record of the names, or if there was a special reason for the photograph. However, it is interesting if only to study the elaborate fashionable hairstyles and the style of everyday dress of the time.

Lipton's, Elgin High Street, 1930s. 'I mind the wooden floor they had there. Next door was Asher's the draper – another shop with a wooden floor – and with one of those pulley-pots you put your money in an' a bittie later it would come back with your change.' The staff gather outside with the message boy and his bike in the pre-salmonella days of shillings, half-crowns and ha'pennies.

The butcher's shop of William Geddes, 182 High Street, Elgin, 1950s. Before shrink-wrapped joints and polystyrene trays with cuts of meat became the supermarket norm, people could see exactly where their meat came from and the condition it was in. Joints were selected and cut to the exact requirements of the individual customer. In this picture Angus Geddes is adjusting the window display.

Lachie, March 1888. In spite of her elaborate hairstyle and fashionable hat, the woman remains anonymous. The subject of the picture, and obviously highly regarded as befits such a character, is Lachie, alert and ready to tackle anything.

The Macrae brothers, 1932. These were meal and grain merchants until 1970. In this picture the staff gather outside, admiring the Morris Commercial van on the cobbled street in the days when there was two-way traffic either side of St Giles'. On the right can be seen the British Linen Bank, supposedly once the site, in pre-Reformation days, of the ground and gardens of the vicar of St Giles' Manse.

Office at the turn of the century. This is believed to be the office, at the back of Cooperie Fraser's Close, of James Jessiman, carpenter and a keen photographer. He did a lot of work at Gordonstoun, St Columba's Church and at Pluscarden Priory in the 1900s. Many young men from his family emigrated around this time. Four brothers went to the Klondyke and one to Australia. Another relative, thought to be the young man in the photograph, went out to the sugar plantations in Cuba, coming home to fight in the First World War and then returning to Cuba to settle.

A rare occasion, 1966. Colleagues at Stewart & McIsaac gather to commemorate sixty-five years of work by Robert Cruickshank, chief clerk. Standing, from left to right: W.D.G. Chalmers, Norma Dean, Ian Cameron, Rosemary Ross, W. Clark, M. Campbell, G.M. Spence. Seated: Joyce Murray, Mrs B. Neish, Miss Winifred Cruickshank, Robert, Vivienne Abbott, Joan Potts.

Townswomen's Guild afternoon 'do' in the Gordon Arms Hotel, mid-1950s. Although taking place in the afternoon, this event attracted a large audience. In the front row are Mrs Shearer and Mrs Hutcheon, who admitted to taking time off work at H.B. Macintosh's to attend this event.

Riding the Marches. This ceremony is still enacted every two years. As can be seen by the different emblems on their aprons, the men represent the six different Elgin Trades – the Glovers, Hammermen, Tailors, Shoemakers, Weavers and Squarewrights – which formed the Incorporated Trades of Elgin. The Reform Act of 1832 brought many changes, but the part of the Muir of Elgin that the Convenery had acquired from the town in 1760 could not be alienated. New Elgin was founded there and the annual revenue divided between the six craft incorporations.

Pansport and the brewery, 1905. By this time many of the brewery buildings only dated from the fire of 1898. In 1912 the town bought the property for £700, and demolished it to reveal the present view of the cathedral.

Elgin High Street. The days of barefoot boys, before the motor car dominated the cobbled street.

NEEPS, TATTIES & HAYMAKING

O ne of the first things apparent when looking at photographs of farming years ago is the number of individuals required to work the land. The squads of workers, the horses with their attendant horsemen and the essential local smiths were gradually replaced by machinery. The farming communities irrevocably faded away. Between 1960 and 1970 the number of people working on the land halved.

Ready to start hoeing, possibly 1940s. Many men were once employed on the farms, either as regular or temporary workers. Tasks that once required scores of workers are now managed by just a few men with the aid of chemical weedkillers, fertilizers and modern machinery.

Hoeing neeps before the Second World War. Hoeing the neeps was essential to keep weeds from choking the young crop. This back-breaking task was made easier by good 'crack' and fine weather. There is some confusion between turnips and swedes south of the border. *Brassica napus* is the sweet orange turnip, or neep, that traditionally accompanies haggis, but this is commonly known as swede south of the border and has only been recorded since the seventeenth century. *Brassica rapa*, commonly called turnip, has white flesh and has been popular since Roman times.

Carting home the neeps, 1930s. Originally imported to Scotland as a cleaning crop in the eighteenth century, neeps were used as a winter feed for beasts. Before the introduction of neeps the animals were dreadfully weak after their poor winter diet. Farmers and crofters would often have to help their neighbours lift animals up on to their feet before the beasts could be put out to the spring grass. Neeps and hay made a vast improvement to the diet of the beasts, and soon the mills, once used to crush whins for feed, fell redundant.

Tattie planting, before the Second World War. Work that can be done now by one man and a machine once required scores of hands. The drills are ready, and the squad of men are about to plant the seed tatties.

An early tractor, possibly before the First World War. The thin wheels are rapidly getting clogged with soil, but working with this International Farmall tractor is obviously preferable to the old-fashioned horse-drawn method of lifting tatties. In the background women are busy with the back-breaking task of collecting the crop.

Tattie lifting squad, 1930s. At tattie-lifting time squads of casual workers would earn a small wage as they helped to harvest the crop. Autumn school holidays – the tattie holidays – were timed to coincide with the harvest, enabling pupils to take part in what was a major rural community activity and perhaps also earn a few pennies. This group could well be used to illustrate a Lewis Grassic Gibbon novel.

Spraying the crop, 1940s. This Case tractor is pulling an early sprayer, possibly full of distillery waste, used to feed the growing crop.

Bagging tatties, 1940s. Bagging the tatties at Linkwood farm with farmer Iain Robertson helping out as well as supervising.

The tattie-dresser, 1930s. The edge of a wooden cart is just visible to the left, and on the right the baskets used to lift the tatties can be seen. The men in the front are holding the specialized fork, known as a grape.

Tattie-dressing, possibly 1930s. Potatoes have been grown in Scotland since the seventeenth century, becoming a dietary staple by the late eighteenth century. Some commentators of those times believed the introduction of the potato to be of more importance than the steam engine. When the oat crop failed the potato saved the people from famine. Thanks to modern disease-resistant potatoes and modern farming techniques, very few people today have ever seen a case of potato blight.

The workers at Linkwood, early 1900s. The kettle is given prominence and the lad sitting on the bench is cutting off an enormous wad of bread — with a saw! The small man in the doorway could well be the grieve as he has the distinction of a pocket-watch on a chain. They all have cheery, smiling faces; even the man on the far left, holding the grape, is smiling behind his enormous moustache.

Leitchestown farm, 1927. It was during drain-digging in the grounds of this farm in 1816 that the Celtic war trumpet, now known as the Deskford Carnyx, was discovered. It is one of only five known fragments of a carnyx and the discovery of this masterpiece of Celtic craftsmanship has resulted in further recent investigations of the site. It is unlikely that the people pictured here were fully aware of the importance of the land they worked, or that their farm was once a major site for ancient gatherings and ceremonies more than 2,000 years ago.

Harvesting in the Park, Garmouth, 1900. The gentleman in the smart hat is James Spence, grandfather of George Marshall Spence. He is supervising the harvest on what is now the Lemanfield housing estate. Sheaves were gradually fed from the conical stack into the mill by men who can be seen standing in a special well on top of the machine. If the sheaves were not fed in correctly, the revolving drum could be damaged. If not saved by the well, the men ran the risk of falling into the revolving drum of the mill and losing a hand or limb. The straw went up the elevator and on to the 'strae soo'. Special bags, often collected from the railway station or the nearby grain merchants, were used to bag the grain, usually 2 or 2¼ cwt, before it was despatched by rail.

Harvesting with steam traction at the turn of the century. The mill would be fed from the stack and then shifted along to the next stack. Sometimes the threshing would be done in the farmyard, where the sheaves of oats or barley would be brought to the mill. There the 'lousers', usually women, would cut the binding around the sheaves using special lousing knives. These knives were strapped to their hand to prevent them being dropped into the mill. The man feeding the sheaves into the mill could be at risk from the sharp lousing knives. A threshing mill could work several small crofts in one day, the contractors receiving ample supplies of food and drams from each customer. In 1913 it cost £2 a day to hire the threshing mill and engine, or 5s an hour for small crofts. The mill would be moved between several smaller crofts – sometimes as many as six in one day.

Taking home the harvest, 1930s. In 1896 a similar wagon-load of hay caught fire when it passed under a gas lamp and was totally destroyed. Strong horses were necessary to pull such heavy loads and their importance in farm life should never be underestimated. Treated well they were invaluable, and the horsemen who cared for them required skill and patience.

Making hay, probably before the Second World War. A tractor has replaced the steam traction engine driving the Garvie threshing mill. In the background the old railway line provides the vital transport link between communities of town and country.

Stacking the hay, 1940s. Small boys were never far from farm activities. The Linkwood distillery chimney looms in the background.

Broadcasting, probably before the Second World War. This squad of workers was about to start sowing seeds by broadcasting. Using both hands they would fling handfuls of seed in a regular motion from side to side as they paced the field. The seed containers which were hung round their necks were called broadcasts and could contain ½ cwt of seed.

Haymaking at Linkwood, First World War. At the end of the war many soldiers were sent out to farms to help with the haymaking before being demobbed. It is not clear what regiment these are serving with, but the cap badges do not appear to be those of the local Seaforths.

Land girl, Second World War. Many women were employed on the farms during the Second World War and their contribution to the war effort was immense. They did the essential work previously done by the menfolk, most of whom had gone off to war.

CHAPTER 4

HORSE POWER & STEAM

Horses were a vital part of life until the petrol engine took over their role. Skilled horsemen were in great demand and a great mystique grew up around them. Those who knew the magical 'horseman's word' were held in great respect. This secret word, when whispered in the ear of a horse, supposedly made it biddable and obedient to the whisperer. Once mechanical horse power appeared, the numerous smithies were replaced by garages and people soon developed new mechanical skills.

The donkey cart at Lemanacre, Garmouth, 1907. The word 'leman' means sweetheart or paramour, and the house was originally built for a much-loved lady many years ago. In the back of the cart are Jean and Polly Spence. Holding the reins is Colin Geddie, who is sitting beside his cousin Jean/Jane Geddie. At the door of the house on the left is Charlotte Spence, and on the right is Barbara Spence. Barbara died not long after this photograph was taken, as a result of a tragic firework accident at Maggie Fair.

Somewhere in Elgin, 1880s. Although the groom is holding the head of this well-bred pair of horses, the lady driver has them well in hand. (It is interesting just how many colloquialisms derive from working with horses.) Bolting horses could cause many serious or even fatal accidents and skill was required to control such animals effectively, especially in a busy town centre.

Outside the Royal Bank of Scotland, Elgin, 143 High Street, probably during the 1880s. The cobbled streets would have ensured quite a bumpy ride even in the well-sprung little pony carriage. As well as the bank and law offices of Stewart & McIsaac, this building housed the office of the Town Clerk. Hugh Stewart, senior partner in the firm of solicitors at 141 High Street, was Town Clerk from 1885 as well as agent for the Royal Bank and eventually became Honorary Sheriff-Substitute and vice-president of the Incorporated Society of Law Agents in Scotland.

Haymaking, First World War. There are three small boys in the picture, all involved in helping with the big horses – at least eleven horses are in use in this photograph. Horses were far more picturesque than the tractor which was soon to replace them, but they all required time to hitch up in the morning. They also needed care after the day's work, as well as frequent attention from the blacksmith. Such a labour-intensive way of life did not last long once the petrol-driven machines appeared.

James Ross at Findrassie farm, 1923. Findrassie was once the seat of the Leslies and there was a fortalice there, but the castle has completely gone. A good stallion, as pictured here, was a valuable beast and would be much in demand by neighbouring farms as a sire. 'My father would walk for miles between farms with the stallion, but they say he left more maids than mares pregnant!' A poem by Flora Garry, 'The Horseman', describes the flurry in the farmhouse caused by the arrival of such a man, Charlie, who 'traivelt a staig'.

Fertilizing the fields, 1930s. Distillery waste is probably being used. Compared with methods today, this would have been very time-consuming and at the end of the day the horse would need to be fed and watered before the horseman could stop work.

Ploughing match, 1960s. Tradition is still kept alive, but nowadays ploughing is a specialist event, with horses groomed and polished and dressed to perfection, a far cry from the past days of regular heavy muddy grinding farm work. Really good horse ploughing is still considered superior to that done with a tractor; however, a semi-skilled man can plough almost ten times more with a tractor in the same time that it takes a skilled man to plough an acre with a pair of horses.

Gordon Castle estate, 1930s. Francis Vass with two of the horses in the stableyard after a hard and muddy day's work. Horses played such a large role in the society of the time that there were many laws and by-laws affecting them. One of the more archaic made it an offence under the Burgh (Police) Scotland Act to lead a stallion through the town, in order to avoid offending delicate sensibilities!

Bob Stewart and Peter Vass making a horse-shoe at one of the several smiddys at Alves. Beating the horseshoe into shape would take skilled and well-practised synchronization between the two of them.

Alternative horse power – Sandy Aitkenhead Junior beside the Reo bus. In 1919 Alexander Aitkenhead was one of the inaugurators of the Elgin bus service, which later became the Grey Line. Three generations of Aitkenheads served on the buses. The splendid vehicle pictured here was a Canadian Reo, capable of doing 70 mph. Unfortunately the speed limit, seen written beside the front wheel arch, was initially 12 mph. This limit was increased to 20 mph, but understandably Sandy made several appearances in Elgin Sheriff Court to pay a £3 speeding fine.

The Grey Line bus, 1930s. The driver is Colin McKay and the conductress May Fraser. A driver's weekly wage was £2 10s, a conductor's was 12s 6d. 'I remember one time when the bus made an unscheduled stop. The driver [not the one pictured here!] had suffered a serious loss the previous evening, following extensive hospitality from various friends. Despondent and fragile, driving his usual route he suddenly remembered everything. Passengers waited patiently while he leapt out, ran across to the nearby fencepost which had supported him the evening before, and retrieved his precious false teeth which he had so carefully placed there!'

Wee Donaldie, the steam engine, 1930s. Taken at the end of Linkwood Road and New Elgin Road, this picture shows Jim Dick (left) and Jimmy Fraser. The road engine hauled two wagons and an 'Elgin County Council' bothy, with a coal wagon behind the bothy. This assembly was still on the go during the Second World War.

A Foden steam lorry at Rothes Glen, 1930s. The crew of this Morayshire County Highways vehicle was again Jim Dick (left) and Jimmy Fraser. At that time, before the premises moved to Ashgrove, the County Council garage was at Thornhill.

Douglas Harper, general merchant of Alves. Here he is serving customer Rosie McLeod at Ardgye, late 1920s. While his wife worked in the shop, Douglas would travel around all the local farms and estates with his horse and cart. Such merchants provided a most essential service for the more isolated country homes.

Postwar grocery delivery van. The writing on the van says 'Phone Whiterashes 29'. Note the very up-to-date Brylcreem hairstyles of Willie and his mate, as well as the long shirt collar with neat tie and trousers with turn-ups.

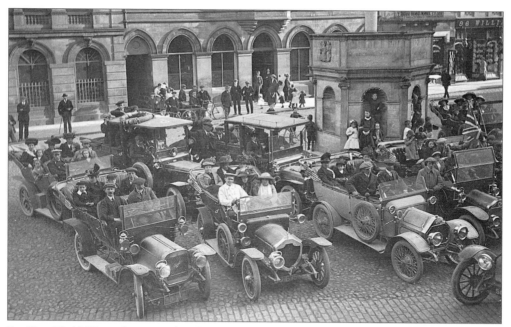

Pre-First World War gathering on the Plainstones. At the front left is an Argyll car, which was Scottish built. Gas lamps can be seen on every car, as well as beaded tyres. Many of the cars pictured are chauffeur driven and all seem to have children in them. The reason for this special occasion is not recorded.

St Leonard's, Duff Avenue, 1935. Mrs A. Low Mustard with her little daughter Muriel beside a Hillman Minx in the days before their home became a hotel. Cars offered more and more freedom and independence to people – especially to the women who were able to enjoy the new technology.

Charlie Spence, late 1920s. An early motor bike enthusiast, Charlie was killed, soon after this photograph was taken, as a result of a motor bike accident. Although she eventually married and had a family of her own, his girlfriend Elsie always kept this photo of him.

Alan Harper, 1950s. A more primitive machine can just be seen in the background, but in those days the tricycle was every young boy's dream – before his thoughts turned to bicycles and motor bikes. In the days before 'trainers', Clark's sandals were considered the sensible summer footwear for children.

Milk delivery, 1953. W. Gregson is working for Allarburn dairy in the days before the electric floats. A fine job on a sunny June morning like this, it was no fun in the depths of winter – but at least there was the horse to talk to!

Charlie Scott of Brigeyn with his van, 1950s. The Town Clerk, Harold Tait, granted Charlie Scott a renewal of his slaughterman's licence for the princely sum of 1s on condition that it would be renewed annually. When his move was made to the new slaughterhouse he would be required to return the licence for amendment 'as the new Slaughterhouse will be equipped with additional slaughtering instruments'.

CHAPTER 5

HIGH CLIMBERS

The Moray Mountaineering Club was founded in 1932 with the aim of 'encouraging mountaineering; to serve as a bond of union amongst lovers of the Scottish hills'. The annual subscription was 5*s* for senior members, 2*s* 6*d* for sixteen to eighteen-year-old juniors. Members from all areas of Elgin society were drawn together by their common love of the mountains. The president in 1935, J. Geddes, member of the Scottish Mountaineering Club, was a renowned amateur pianist and was on the advisory council of the BBC. He adjudicated at piano competitions and was the organizer of Elgin Chamber Music club. He once managed to persuade his friend Myra Hess, the famous pianist, and the vocalist Elizabeth Schumann to perform locally.

Ethel Fraser in 1920 before she joined the Moray Mountaineering Club. Ethel Fraser was a book-keeper at the Elgin Dairy, and was one of the small group of intrepid ladies who enjoyed many excursions with the club. To accompany her photographs she wrote several evocative descriptions of these early days in the Scottish hills. Thanks to these careful records it is possible to share some of those experiences with her, in spite of the distance in time between us.

Moray Mountaineering Club on Mealfourvanie, 20 October 1946. Walking and mountaineering rapidly became favourite and relatively inexpensive activities. Clubs offered a means of easy access to the great outdoors for people with transport difficulties. After the war there was a growing appreciation of the countryside and the feeling of freedom found in the hills. Novices could soon learn mountaineering skills from the more experienced enthusiasts who led the groups. Boot studs are well in evidence here, while tweed skirts rather than trousers were still the normal gear for the ladies.

The Moray Mountaineering Club displaying their renowned sartorial elegance, 1930s. A disappointingly small meet was recorded on a very rainy 16 October 1933 when the walk was in the Cabrach, via the Buck and several other hills. The Grouse Inn provided tea for 1s per head and a fountain pen was presented then to J.C. Ewan, one of the earlier members. A rowing 'blue' of Cambridge University, he was a maths teacher at Elgin Academy and was leaving for Edinburgh to become secretary to the Scottish Council of School Broadcasting. Two years later he was killed in a climbing accident in the Swiss Alps.

Ed Davidson, the Moray Mountaineering Club secretary in the 1930s. The club leaflet of December 1933 advised members on suitable clothing to wear on outings. This included 'a woollen vest, flannel shirt, pullover, woollen scarf, balaclava helmet, windproof blouse or jacket, 2 pairs of woollen gloves, outer windproof gloves are useful, underpants, plus fours or breetches – not tight at knees – 2 pairs stockings, boots – correctly nailed with inner cork sole.'

Moray Mountaineering Club Annual General Meeting, followed by dinner, at the Station Hotel, Elgin, Saturday 23 February 1935. Committee members, back row, left to right: R. Stobbart, G. Thomson, I. MacDonald, T. Crowley, E. Davidson (hon. secretary and treasurer). Front row: Rector of Elgin Academy, H. Humble (vice-president), Mae McBain, Miss H. Harrison (vice-president), J. Geddes (president), Ethel Fraser, F. MacKenzie (hon. president). Ethel wrote in her diary: 'First we had our Annual General Meeting, getting through the business in record time . . . & Mr. Stobbart and I were elected to the committee. The address and lantern lecture by Mr Adam was an absolute treat. He held us all spellbound and I was very sorry when he finished. His slides were magnificent. I only wish we had time to see more of them.'

That same evening. From the left: John Geddes, J. MacDonald, F. MacKenzie, R. Stobbart, T. Crowley. Ethel recorded, 'Before we adjourned for dinner the Committee were photographed, also some of the men intently gazing at a map. The dinner passed off very well indeed, we had a merry time. Mr A.B. Simpson gave us a very racy speech which was much enjoyed. We had Mr & Mrs Burr singing to us, and we felt quite sorry when the evening finished off about 12.30.' The menu consisted of 'Cream of Cairntoul soup, Loch Affric trout with Snow Cornice sauce, Mutton from the Shepherds Hill (Meall Bhuchaille), Glenmore roast (but not carved by the President), Potatoes – Crowley's Golden Wonders, peas – Garnets of Sgurr nan Ceathreamhan.' The sweets were listed as 'Meaghaidh-Mist by the secretary, The Delicate Trifles – the Ladies of our Club,' and finally 'A "Humble" savoury – "Finlay" on toast, Cafe a la Cromdale – but tea for the Treasurer if he is not lost.'

All-night crossing of the Lairig Ghru, by Miss Hood, Ethel Fraser, Bess Anderson and Rita Fraser, Saturday 2 July 1938. Ethel records in her diary: 'At last I have accomplished a long-wished for desire – to walk through the Lairig Ghru.' They left Elgin on the 2.20 train, reaching Aberdeen shortly after 5 p.m., where they had tea before going by bus to Braemar. They set off from Braemar at 8.45 p.m.

'Here we watched a fisher for a short time, read the notice to litter-louts and then proceeded to our grand adventure.' They reached Derry Lodge at midnight.

'We now had our supper and then lay down on the heather and had a rest for an hour. It was a warm night with only an occasional suggestion of a breeze. We appeared to have chosen an ant-hill on which to sleep.'

They then passed through a wood – ' . . . rather dark and eerie, had it not been for our torches we could hardly have found our way. At last however, we were through the wood, and over the stream to where the path divides for Lairig Ghru and Lairig an Loaigh. It was now fairly dark but we carried on till 2 a.m. and the bridge over the Luibeg Burn. Here again we rested for an hour beside some gaunt, dead trunks of trees which looked as if they were relics of some battlefield. When we rose this time day had broken and we had no difficulty in finding the path. What an experience it was walking through those desolate deserted acres with never a sign of a human being, in the early hours of a lovely morning.' Breakfast was at 4 a.m. opposite Corrour bothy, where they saw several deer in the early morning mist.

'Then over those awful boulders to the Pools of Dee, clear and icy, and most refreshing after our long trudge. Rita and I toasted John in the water, for with him we made our first acquaintance of these pools. Then we came past the March Burns to the summit of the pass. Miss Hood took some snapshots and we lingered long, looking down into the lovely valley of Rothiemurchas. By now the sun was quite high and the effect on the Rainbow screes of Ben Macdhui was simply wonderful. I could not tear my eyes from them and was forever missing my footholds. Where the path crosses the stream for the last time we lay down on the rocks and had a sleep, to be awakened by rain, but this shower soon passed and we came at last to that delightful grassy spot by the Cairngorm footbridge. All those long miles this grassy place had been in my mind as the place where it would be delightfully soft to lie and slumber, but no sooner had we got settled than a terrific thunder show came on and we were forced to find shelter under the trees. Now we made for Coylum and Mrs Garrow's where we received every hospitality, such as dinner and then BED to sleep for 12 solid hours.' They then walked the 2 miles to Aviemore station to catch the train home to Elgin.

Moray Mountaineering Club, weekend in the Cairngorms, 14 April 1935. From the left: Miss McBain, Mr Dawson, Lt-Col Butchart, Mr Stobbart, Rita Fraser. The club rented Glenmore lodge, owned by the Forestry Commission. Members provided their own bed linen and towels and the club arranged for a lorry to take members' luggage to the lodge at a charge of 1s per member.

The Cairn, Ben Macdhui, 4,296 ft, Sunday, 23 July 1933. Ethel and friends set off at 9 a.m. and walked to just above the tree line where they stopped for lunch. 'Immediately after lunch we started to climb – it was pretty stiff going, especially the first part up to the Lurcher's Crag. On the way Mr Davidson gave us a lesson in map and compass reading – but I'm afraid I'll need some further lessons before I become anything like proficient. We reached the summit at 2 p.m., having taken 5 hours from Coylumbridge, where we had some snaps taken.' Ethel then goes on to describe the wonderful views and she noted with relief that, 'In spite of some showers on the way down, the ladies didn't need to change their stockings.' They arrived home at 11 p.m. after 'a great day'.

Ethel Fraser and Beatrice Ogilvie outside Glenmore Lodge, with ice axes, during the Moray mountaineering weekend in the Cairngorms, 15 April 1935. During this weekend Ethel was at last able to record 'We decided to go and have a look at Loch Aron, on doing so could not resist going down all the way, so at last I have been to the famous Shelter Stone. Unfortunately the book could not be found, so I was unable to record my visit.' Ethel enjoyed several good walks, in spite of slipping and 'glissading, tumbling and rolling down about 100ft' when she was traversing the slope of Coire Cas during the return from the summit of Cairngorm. 'It was a horrible sensation and I thought my last hour had come. However, I finally managed to pull up with the aid of the ice-axe which fortunately the President had handed to me a few minutes before. When they saw I had slipped they shouted down to me not to move, and they came down and the rope was put to use again. I wasn't hurt at all but felt my bruises the next day alright.' The next day, undaunted, 'Beatrice, David and I set off for the Ryroan Bothy.' She records, 'A great weekend, everything passed off successfully, everybody seemed happy and we are all home safe and sound once more. David christened us the "Elks" – Elderly Ladies Knitting Society!'

CHAPTER 6

WAR

Many of Elgin's young men fought and died in foreign fields in several wars. Years of peace blunt some memories, but it is impossible to overestimate the effects of death and of disability on those who did return. No one returns from carnage unscathed, and those left at home also had their lives irrevocably changed. Memories of glory and comradeship must be tempered with the realities of pain, maiming and bereavement. In spite of the horrors, there have been many tales of quiet unsung heroism, brave acts performed by ordinary men and women. Elgin has many such heroes, but some of their stories may never be heard.

James Brander Dunbar, during the Boer War (1899–1902). While his colleague carries a whip, Capt Dunbar, wearing a mourning band, carries an assegai, a slender native spear made of hard wood and tipped with iron. During this war the British lost 28,000 men, the Boers lost 4,000, but over 26,000 Boer civilians died of disease in the British concentration camps, as did thousands of native people.

Donald Robertson in the First World War. Donald did return home, but remained badly affected by the mustard gas he had encountered. Returning soldiers did not always receive the help they needed. Typically, a survivor of the Battle of Balaclava (1854) was told that his services were not sufficient to entitle him to a pension from the War Office. Thanks to the writings of some who experienced the First World War, people began to have some slight understanding of what had been endured by thousands of British soldiers far afield.

A group of cheery Seaforths during, or just after, the First World War. They are not dressed for battle and this photograph would appear to have been taken with the object of reassuring the folks back home that their lads were well fed and happy. Nailed boots are very much in evidence. Presumably they had just set up camp as one lad is still clutching the tent peg hammer. The mess cans are clearly visible and the soldier sitting on the right is cleaning his plate with his 'piece', while his neighbour pours something from a bottle into his comrade's mug.

The Seaforth TA, C Company, winners of inter-company tug-of-war, 1924. Various amalgamations in 1881 between Highlander regiments (72 and 78), the Highland Rifle Militia and the Volunteer Battalions of Ross, Sutherland, Caithness and Moray formed the new Seaforth Regiment. Nineteen battalions of Seaforths served in the First World War in Macedonia, Palestine, Mesopotamia and on the Western Front.

Kilt-makers in the Drill Hall, Elgin, 1914/15. Making kilts for the Seaforths, these originally non-combatant tailors were soon to see action on the front as the war machine devoured more and more men.

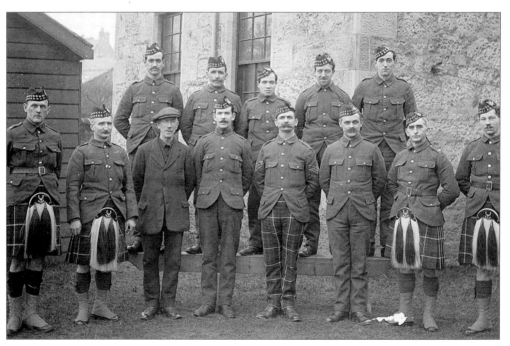

The kilt-makers of the Seaforths outside the Drill Hall, Elgin, 1914/15. There are still people in their eighties who treasure special family pictures which belonged to some of these men. The pictures were returned, blood-stained and shrapnel-pierced, among the paltry possessions of fathers, sons and brothers who perished in the First World War, leaving behind children who never knew them.

William Robertson at the Palace. For his work in the First World War William received an OBE. He had been in Canada as a veterinary surgeon and returned to Britain to care for horses during the war. Note the maple-leaf cap badge. Thousands of horses were commandeered for war work and many were killed in the carnage. Work done by vets such as William Robertson would have been traumatic, but would have helped to alleviate much suffering. Accompanying him to Buckingham Palace were his sister Mabel and his mother.

Wedding group at Fleurs House just after the First World War. So many men never returned from war that weddings were very special occasions. This is believed to be the wedding of Maj. James Gregory Birnie Gordon, born in India in 1881, the son of Capt. J.L.J. Gordon. This Maj. Gordon served in South Africa, India and Mesopotamia and was shot through the knee. He was an officer in the Indian Army and was awarded the Military Cross in 1902 and 1916.

Members of the Polish Regiment during the Second World War, planning for the French D-Day landings. On the right, smoking a cigarette, is Tomasz Kozlowski, who later settled in Elgin, married his Elgin sweetheart and worked in Bilbohall hospital until he retired. Forced out of their homeland and witness to many atrocities of war, the Polish forces would not give up the battle and were renowned for their ferocious determination. If they had run out of ammunition, Polish pilots attached to the RAF would desperately ram their own machines into the enemy rather than withdraw from the battle.

Marie Young, an Elgin quine, working in the war. The Second World War changed attitudes and working practices and many women learnt hitherto undreamed-of new skills. Here is a local girl, with her contemporary hairstyle, working in an RAF radio station with some of the state-of-the-art equipment.

A break in the war effort. Many people remember not only the horrors and uncertainties of the Second World War, but also the camaraderie – and the endless cups of tea at every opportunity. Marie Young was one of many women who worked in radio operations and this picture of her radio station comrades typifies a quiet moment of relaxation in the Nissen hut.

Home Guard, 1941. Thought to have been taken outside the Drill Hall in the Cooper Park, this is a photograph of some of the local men who made up the Elgin Home Guard. Some of them had undoubtedly served in the First World War and, in spite of age, were willing to serve again to the best of their abilities to protect their country. Secret ammunition caches were stored in the countryside, such as the one that used to be in the wood at Cranloch. These caches were kept ready for use in guerrilla action should the enemy manage to penetrate as far as Moray. Now hardly a trace remains of their existence.

CHAPTER 7

CHILDHOOD

From an early age children used to be treated as young adults, most having to take some responsibilities within the family. Spending power was very limited and teenagers did not exist as a separate species until after the Second World War. One of the most obvious differences apparent in old photographs is the restrictive and difficult-to-clean clothing of the old days. In 1887, following an incident when two odoriferous small boys had been sent home from school, it was agreed at a parish council meeting that tweeds should be substituted for the moleskins and velveteen worn by the pauper children. The offenders were not to return until the foul-smelling garments had been washed. Years later small boys wore short trousers, not for aesthetic reasons but because knees were far more resilient to rough and tumble than the relatively expensive cloth of the day!

Milne's Institute, Fochabers, 1910. Alexander Milne was born in the mid-eighteenth century. A servant in Gordon Castle, he was dismissed for refusing to cut his fashionable peruke hairstyle. He made his fortune in America, leaving $100,000 to Fochabers for educational purposes, and Milne's Institute was erected in 1846. The names of the children in the photograph are not recorded. Some of the jumpers worn by the boys are 'more holey than righteous', contrasting with the perfectly attired child in the sailor suit (right). The girls show a variety too, from lace and pintucks to practical smocks.

Elgin Academy 5th year, 1946. Many 'weel kent' faces here. Back row, from left to right: Hamish Sim, James Falconer, Robin Stewart, Ian Taylor, Tony ?, Ashley Buchan, -?-, -?-, Ian Machardie. Middle row: John Taylor, Gordon George, Teddy Strachan, David Lang, Eileen Bisset, Barbara Thomson, Mildred Mackenzie, -?-, Roy McLennan, Leslie Roy, Gordon Catto. Front row: Margaret Robertson, Moira Mackenzie, Oonah Taylor, Elizabeth Burn, Sheena Forbes, Netta Watt, Lydia MacLennan, Betty Mackenzie, Muriel Mustard, Beth Sutherland, Lorna Jamieson.

Studio portrait, 1880s. Their names are not recorded, but this portrait reveals a lot about the subjects' life-style at the time. The young woman is neatly clad in leather gloves with beautiful frills showing under her dress. Her fashionable, neatly pinched waist is doubtless at least partly the result of a good, boned corset. The proper upkeep of all their restrictive clothes would require much hard work. Both children are wearing button boots, which required a special button-hook to fasten efficiently. The child on the right wears neatly darned woollen stockings.

Wee Jean Eddie, mid-1930s. A snowy day and wee Jean is well happit with her bunnet, fur gloves and button gaiters. She is the granddaughter of the lady with the splendid hat on page 115.

James Brander Dunbar, 1879. Taken on his fourth birthday, this photograph shows a typical pose of the day, the young laird seated on a fur, holding a gun, portent of a far from dull future. The little button-up boots have been beautifully polished.

Geordie and James Roy Peterkin, 1922. In their button shoes and bloomers, these two loons are playing with replicas of a steam traction engine and steam train, the giants of their day. Two generations later such young boys would take the family car for granted. Since the days when steam was king man has reached for the stars and the silicon chip controls the world.

Mrs Arbuthnot Dunbar and family at Newton House, 1891. Mother Katie, properly attired in gloves as befits a lady, holds her son Edward on her lap while her oldest son Arbuthnot, wearing his sailor suit, sits on the table. Her seven daughters pause from their game of tennis to pose for the photographer. A friend of the family is seated on the tricycle.

Boarding school cricket group, late 1890s. Families who could afford it sent their sons away to boarding school for their education. Friends and connections made at these prestigious schools would often have a major influence on the boys' future life. This is a group of schoolboys at Ardvreck, which was attended by some of the Dunbar family.

George, James Roy and Alfred, 1926. Three loons ready for trouble! This was taken at The Plots, land rented out as allotments at Borough Briggs, where the new leisure centre is now. The Haugh garages are visible in the background.

Marie and Nanny, 1926. Nannies were an invaluable addition to a busy household, providing stability and regular routine for their demanding small charges while busy parents could concentrate on other important affairs.

Unidentified grandmother proudly displaying her offspring, 1920s. Since 1918, when women over thirty were allowed to vote, grandmothers have changed. No longer the often austere-looking matriarchs wearing black dresses and smelling of lavender water and mothballs, today's grandmothers are likely to sport multi-coloured leggings and smell of aromatherapy products, but their essential function remains the same. They must act as a bridge between generations and a point of stability in the confusing world of childhood. The rewards are unchanged – the pleasure of indulging in the fascinating world of children for a while, then returning them to their parents!

Mildred and Jim Robertson, being prepared, 1937. Note the perfectly polished shoes. Often polishing the family shoes was one of the regular chores of children. When Lord Baden-Powell called the first groups of Boy Scouts to a meeting in London in 1910 he was faced with a small but determined group of girls who had accompanied their brothers. The girls insisted they too wanted to join and so Miss Agnes Baden-Powell was drafted in to help form the Girl Guides. During the First World War Guides helped in many ways, including in canteens, hospitals and first aid stations.

Elgin Scouts getting the trek cart ready before setting out for camp, 1935/6. The Boy Scout movement was founded in 1908 by Sir Robert Baden-Powell. In 1910 he retired from the army to devote his time to the organization. In 1936 the Scouts totalled 2,510,000, over a million being in the then British Empire. The future before the Elgin Scouts in this photograph was very varied: some died young, one of them became a squadron leader, another a doctor.

Second Elgin, East End Scouts, 1935/6. Back row, left to right: Hugh Ross, Lewis Leslie, Alex Wilson, Ronnie Cameron, Stan Watson, George Ferguson, Eddie Mackenzie, Sandy Watson. Middle row: Henry Macdonald, Robert Hardie, Harry Watson, George Grant, Ian Rose, Don Ferguson, Sandy Reid, Colin Milne, Frank Simpson. Front row: Hamish Macdonald, Ian Hardie, John Tonge, Pat Anderson, Jimmy Falconer, Hamish Hay, Sandy Macdonald, Jimmy Cameron. The three Macdonalds are brothers, as are the three Watsons, the two Hardies and the two Fergusons.

Relugas Guide camp, 1926. Some things hardly change. Since Guides began emulating the Scouts, young girls have been setting up camp and sleeping under canvas with varying degrees of enthusiasm. Equipment has improved over the years, and the intensity of anticipation and the excitement of successful occasions have ensured that this kind of activity will continue to remain popular. Hope continues to triumph over many adverse experiences!

Carefree days in Guide camp, 1936. Supping soup out of their enamel mugs. The guider was Margaret Turner, who later married the architect John Wright. Also in the picture is Elsie MacDonald, sister of George and John, who both followed in their father's footsteps and became much-respected local GPs in Elgin.

A French picnic, Covesea caves, 1934. These 5th form girls from the Academy were enjoying a cycle excursion to the beach and during the outing were only allowed to speak French. Back row, left to right: Freda Middleton, Doreen Knox, Morag Matheson, Jean Stuart, Frances Masson, Jean Milne, Chrissie MacPherson, Cathie Cockburn, Winnie Gordon, Ella Davidson, Molly Forsyth, Alice Maclennan. In front: Rita Ross, Elma Sawyer, Lily Morrice.

Alan and Neil, 1950s. These two small boys are playing outside the 'prefabs', at Cameron Road, Bishopmill. Prefabs, built to ease the postwar housing shortage, are remembered with varying degrees of affection by their many tenants and often sheltered families for many more years than was originally intended.

CHAPTER 8

DRESSING UP & DRESSING DOWN

Most Elgin folk are very sociable and throughout its recent history the town has always had a good selection of clubs and societies to cater for all interests. Folk in Elgin are not averse to the sartorial challenge presented by sporting activities. Bunnets, toories and top hats have always been worn with equal aplomb, while the challenge of dressing up for special occasions has been tackled with gusto.

Waiting for Queen Victoria to pass through, Tuesday 6 September 1872. The Queen was on her way to Dunrobin Castle and the train stopped from 1.58 p.m. until 2.03 p.m. The band played, the assembled populace cheered and Queen Victoria waved graciously from her carriage. Close examination of the photograph reveals an enormous turnout. The archway has been specially garlanded for the important five minutes. Loyal subjects are even sitting on roofs to obtain a good view of the proceedings on this special occasion.

The royal visit to Elgin, 14 August 1961. Elgin's Lady Provost, Miss I. Duncan, is on the left. Miss Duncan's memorable election slogan was 'don't talk bunkum, vote for Duncan'. Behind her is, on the far left, Kenny McKessack and Brig. Sir Henry Holdsworth, Lord Lieutenant of Moray. Lady Holdsworth is on the steps beside the Lady-in-Waiting, who is holding the umbrella. Andrew Thomson, County Clerk, is in the doorway.

The royal visit, 1961. Lined up outside the Court House, waiting to meet the Queen, from the right: The Laird of Pitgaveny, Capt. James Brander Dunbar DL; Brig. I.K. Thomson DL; John Brodie, former Provost of Elgin; F.O. Stuart DL; Capt. Iain Tennant DL; -?-; Gordon Campbell MP; William Munro, former Provost of Elgin; -?-; -?-; the Revd N.W. Sammon; John N. Petrie, Vice-Convenor of Moray.

Dallas fête, beside Dallas school, before the First World War. In the background people are dancing, while on the right of the picture the swings are being put to energetic use.

The wedding of Mary Adam at Amberley, Mayne Road, 1913. The minister standing second from the right is the Revd Mr McPherson (featured on page 83 of *Elgin in Old Photographs*). The groom is Dr William Anderson, the best man, William Adam, is standing behind the bride on her left and standing beside him is Dorothy Robertson. Alex Adam of Kinneddar is third from the right in the back row. The ladies, seated, from the left: May Grant, Jessie Merson, Jeannie Robertson, Nellie Leitch, Mable Robertson, the bride's mother, Mena Sim, -?-, -?-, Penelope Leitch.

Taken at the end of the last century this photograph is of an unnamed sister of H.B. Macintosh. The hairstyle is incredibly elaborate with a fashionable 'Spanish comb' holding it in place. It must have been very heavy to wear and would have required carefully restrictive posture to maintain!

Unknown special occasion at the end of the last century. The names, the place and the occasion have long been forgotten, but judging by the dresses and hats this was a special day. Perhaps the young girl in the white dress was celebrating her birthday or engagement.

Outside the Old Town Hall, at the beginning of the century. At one of the hugely popular fancy dress parties often held there, the girls are dressed to represent the countries of the British Empire and the world. Margaret Fordyce, eldest daughter of the painter William Fordyce, is fourth from the left in the middle row. She married John Ross in 1911, who is pictured opposite.

Fancy dress, 1920s. Jean McLeod in costume for a fancy dress ball at the Assembly Rooms. People loved dressing up and there was great fascination with all things Oriental in the 1920s and 1930s. Enormous trouble was taken with costumes for the dances and parties, as shown here, even down to the satin shoes with button fastenings.

The Elgin Twenty Club, session 1909–10. This was one of the six Elgin debating societies at the time (distinct from the National Twenty Club which was a shooting club). Back row, left to right: J.C. Grant (secretary), J. Anderson, A.J. Morrison, J. Black, J. Sutherland, W. Fraser. C. Hutcheson, J. Ross. Middle row: G. Grant, G. Robertson, W. Hossack, D. Campbell, J. Manson (president), J. Anderson. Front row: R.D. Stewart, J. Wilson, R. Stephen, W. Anderson.

John Ross (top right) was born in Old Deer in 1885 and moved to Elgin in 1908. In 1911 he married Margaret Fordyce, eldest daughter of William Fordyce, painter. They emigrated to Canada where he worked as a grocer. He died of heart failure on a golf course in 1920.

A report in the *Northern Scot*, December 1910, describes the 'At Home' held by the Elgin Twenty Club in the Gordon Arms Hotel. Over thirty couples were present and a successful evening of dance was enjoyed until 2 a.m.

Elgin Wheelers Cycling Club, 1934, long before lycra-assisted aerodynamics contributed to enjoyment of the sport! 'Curly' Thom, third from right, came third in this North of Scotland event. It was not uncommon for young men of the time to cycle home to Elgin from college or university in Aberdeen at weekends – but then, of course, the roads were much quieter.

New Elgin 'Bullwhackers', New Year Day, 1909. It is believed that this was a 'one-off' gathering of football enthusiasts for a special game. Back row, left to right: James Reid, John Menzies (referee), William Bain, John Younie, John Asher, James Walker, Thomas Davidson, John Smith, George Ogilvie, John J. Hay, Robert Cruickshank, William Gordon. Middle row: Robert Grant, William Culbard, James Garden (captain), Alex Pirie, William Clunas. Front row: John Mackenzie, Alex Falconer. Robert Cruickshank served sixty-five years with the firm of Stewart & MacIsaac and is featured on page 28.

The rugby players, 1940s. Back row, second from the left, is Roy Tulloch. Middle row, from left to right: Dr John MacDonald, Stan Williamson, Morton Stevens, Taffy Watts, Bill Ettles. Front row, on the right, is Robbie Anderson, and next to him John Grigor.

Elgin City County Cricket 2nd XI, 1911. Some strangers to the district have expressed surprise to learn that cricket is not confined to south of the border! In 1914 the Elgin pitch was regarded as the best north of Aberdeen and was recorded as having 'turned out many a fine team for fully a half century'. The captain sitting in the centre of the front row is Jim Grigor.

Moray & Nairn Unionist Ball at the Assembly Rooms, Elgin, 1948/50. Standing, left to right: Mrs Mary Welsh, Willie Welsh, -?-, George Spence, George Douglas, -?-. Seated: Mrs Jean Philip (later Ferreira), Mrs Bunty Bannerman, Mrs Simpson, Miss Alice Anderson, Mrs Alex Spence, Mr J.Y. Philip.

Maryhill curling pond, Oldmill Road, 1965. On the left is Wilfred Adam of Glassgreen, in the white hat is George Spence, and on the right is Gwen Mackay.

Carrie's Dance, in the Assembly Rooms, 1950. William Carrie, third from left in the front row, owned the grocery in Elgin High Street, at the bottom of Commerce Street. He also owned a shop in Lossiemouth which was managed by William Fraser, who took over the Elgin shop when it closed. Lachlan McIntosh was manager of the Elgin shop until it closed when he then bought the Lossie shop. George McMurran and Mary (née Hall), who ran Hall's the greengrocer in South Street, can be seen in the back row, third and fourth from the left.

End of an era – the retirement of Moray County Council officials at the re-organization in 1975. Standing behind their wives, left to right: William Hutchison, County Council Sanitary Inspector; W.F. Lindsay, Director of Education; Andrew Thomson, County Clerk; Norman Pratt, Roads Surveyor; Norman Cowper, Planning Officer.

St Giles' Burns Club Burns Supper, at Murray's Restaurant, 1957. The supper included 'Lossie Sole, weel baned an' Buskit', 'The Haggis wi' Bashed Neeps an' Chappit Tatties' followed by 'A bit o' bonnie Roastit Beef (Calots o' Coo), Tatties warm an' Reekin' wi' Kaleyaird Dainties'. This was followed by sherry trifle 'wi' bangs o' 'ream an' Shouglin' Jeelies forbye', and it was finished off with 'A Farlin o' Oatcake wi' a morsel o' Kebbuck'.

CHAPTER 9

STORIES BEHIND THE FACES

E lgin has its share of characters and interesting stories. Life has never been dull here and folk are willing to accept that human nature has many foibles. While bumptious extroverts are not appreciated, kindly eccentrics are well tolerated and their imperfections accepted – such as the considerate gentleman who had outdoor stairs built to his rooms so that his various visiting lady friends would not disturb the servants. There are many quiet and modest folk, unsung heroes and heroines, who have contributed greatly to the quality of life and influenced our times as well as their own. Here are just a few people who helped shape both the Elgin of today and things further afield.

William Mackie MA, MD, LLD, 1856–1932. An Elgin GP for thirty-five years, Medical Officer of Health for Elgin & Rothes for eighteen years, this modest and retiring man carried out much medical research. Spending leisure time researching geology and minerology, he was elected a fellow of the Edinburgh Geological Society in 1897. In a roadside drystone dyke he discovered the famous Rhynie cherts, containing fossil plants of the Old Red Sandstone era. Interested in sedimentary petrology, he laid the groundwork upon which much of today's modern petro-chemical industry is based. He was a director of the Elgin Literary & Scientific Association, President of the Moray Field Club for fifteen years and President of the Edinburgh Geological Society from 1925 to 1927.

Elgin's first librarian, Miss Isabelle Mitchell, and her assistant. Miss Mitchell was appointed in 1892 and served for thirty-three years. In 1903 she helped to organize a successful Arts and Crafts exhibition to coincide with the opening of the Cooper Park and Grant Lodge. When she retired in 1924 the library in Grant Lodge had expanded to 8,674 volumes in the lending department, 171 in the reference section and 455 in the local collection. She was praised by the Elgin Public Library Committee for 'being most assiduous in connection with the Local Art Gallery and Museum'. She died, aged eighty, in 1934.

Grant Lodge staff, c. 1903. Standing, left to right: W. Robertson, N. Gordon, C.M. Scott, A. Stewart, M.H. Orr, N. Ewan, J. Watt, N. Munn. Seated: J. Dalgarno, W. Brown, W. Donaldson, A. Wilson, I. Mitchell, J. Morrison, J. Middlemass. The public library originally opened in 1892 in a room in the Old Town Hall and moved to Grant Lodge in 1903. The collection originally consisted of 3,366 volumes.

'La Teste', William Hay Leith Teste, born in Crathie in 1829. He was a pageboy at Westerton House, Pluscarden, and derived his name from a French villa where he worked as a valet. He undertook a variety of work from butler to London dockworker. Returning to Elgin 'La Teste' acquired the lease of the Newmarket Inn, then became an under-waiter in the Gordon Arms Hotel but imbibed too well. He produced thirteen editions of his poetry. He arrived at the Poor House, Bishopmill in 1873. As the poet laureate to Lodge Kilmolymock he was buried with full Masonic honours when he died in 1892.

Peter Grant was the kindly governor of Craigmoray, the dreaded Poor House in Bishopmill at the turn of the century. He was sympathetic and kind to 'La Teste', earning his gratitude in 1873 when the impoverished poet found himself destitute. 'La Teste' christened the Poor House 'Peter's Palace' and wrote a poem in appreciation which began:

> Peter, get your palace ready,
> Tak' us a' tae Bishopmill,
> We're hungry, haggart, naket, needy,
> Be thou our good Saint Peter still.

Maj. George Boyd Anderson (1896–1972). This larger than life character was born in Elgin in 1896. His mother was a member of the Johnston family, founders of the famous woollen mill. Maj. Anderson served with the Royal Field Artillery and won the MC in the First World War. He spent time as a rubber merchant in Singapore. A generous benefactor to Moray, he gave money to buy plants for the Cooper Park and gifted the Rose Nursery to Elgin in 1926. He served with the Royal Artillery in the Second World War, afterwards retiring to Skerrybrae, Lossiemouth. Known as 'Lipstick Villa' because of its garish pink paintwork, it contained many idiosyncratic features such as the map of East Asia created in crocus plants on the lawn and a musical toilet seat. In 1956 he presented 160 acres of lochs and gardens, the Millbuies, to Elgin. He was a founder member of the Royal British Legion in Lossiemouth, giving the premises and presenting a pavilion to the town for the playing fields. He funded improvements to the Moray Golf Club course, where he was captain. He donated many interesting items to Elgin Museum, including a whisky smuggler's stick and a tappet hen (a pewter drinking vessel). On moving to Edinburgh in 1957 he gifted his house, Skerrybrae, to be used as a convalescent home. In his will he left instructions that everyone attending his funeral service in Lossiemouth should 'be invited to drink to "my departed spirit" at the Moray Golf Club'.

A distinguished footballer at Everton Football Club, 1913. In the dark goalkeeper's jersey is Frank Mitchell, an Elgin loon. His grandfather, John Mitchell, who died in 1910, was the last of the Elgin Town Drummers, beating the drum at certain times of day and to announce special news. The Town Drum can be seen in the museum. One of a family of ten, Frank was born in Elgin in 1890. His family moved to Glasgow in 1906 where Frank started playing amateur football. Moving to Liverpool in 1913 he made his debut for Everton, making twenty-three appearances. He then played for Liverpool, making eighteen appearances until 1921 when he joined Tranmere Rovers for fifty-five appearances – he was in goal when the famous Dixie Dean first played for that club and was the first man to represent all three Merseyside clubs.

Ramsay MacDonald (1866–1937) at Pitgaveny. The Prime Minister of the first Labour government in Britain is seated on the Bothgowan stone. His brother Malcom stands on the left while the pipe-smoking Laird of Pitgaveny reclines in his kilt. Described as 'too much of a gentleman for politics', Ramsay MacDonald inspired great affection and loyalty in all who worked for him. Owing to his pacifist beliefs he was ejected from membership of the Lossiemouth Golf Club. The Duke of Richmond and Gordon immediately offered him membership of the Spey Bay Golf Club and he never returned to the Lossiemouth club, in spite of later invitations.

Alistair MacDonald and Lord Provost Smith, 28 October 1966. In this photograph Alistair MacDonald, son of Ramsay MacDonald, hands over the President's Badge of the London Morayshire Club for safe-keeping to Lord Provost Smith. From left to right: Harold Tait, Town Clerk, Kelvin MacDonald, Lord Provost Smith, Mrs Isabel Peterkin (daughter of Ramsay MacDonald), Mr Wright, President of the Elgin Society, Alistair MacDonald and his daughter, Mrs Susan Dearman.

Lachlan Mackintosh, of the Old Lodge, father of Herbert (below). A member of the town council until 1888, Convenor of the Six Incorporated Trades, he took an active part in helping to preserve and restore places of historical importance in Elgin, such as the Bishop's Palace. He was instrumental in instigating the search for the Arms of the City and Royal Burgh of Elgin that had been lost and forgotten for centuries, and when the county councils were established in 1890 he designed the official Seal for the county council. He wrote the original *Elgin Past and Present* in 1891.

Herbert B. Macintosh. He was the son of Lachlan Macintosh and, sharing his father's love of the town, in 1914 he compiled an enlarged edition of this most essential history of Elgin and Elginshire. He was the owner of the Woollen Warehouse, originally part of the Old Academy buildings in Francis Place, which was thought to have been built in 1800, partly from materials of the Little Kirk. Some of the carved stones taken from the Little Kirk appeared to have been taken from the cathedral and Herbert incorporated them into a rockery at his house, Redythe.

Sir Archibald Hamilton Dunbar Bart, of Duffus House, JP, Deputy Lieutenant, Captain of the 66th Regiment (1828–1910). A genealogist, he wrote a book about the Scottish kings. The histories of the Dunbar family and of Moray are inextricable. The Records of Elgin state that in 1393 Thomas de Dunbar, Earl of Moray, granted the aldermen, bailies and burgesses of Elgin an exemption of customs upon all the wool, cloth and other things that go by sea 'out of our haven of Spey'. Bishop Columba Dunbar, who died in 1435, is one of many Dunbars buried in the cathedral.

Peter Brown of Dunkinty and Linkwood, known as 'A Farmers' Friend'. The factor on the Seafield estate, he was initially unsympathetic when, following the disruption of the Church in 1843, the Revd Alexander McWatt of Rothes asked for a site for his new manse. Peter, a large imposing man, became increasingly annoyed at the persistent demands of the new Free Church minister, flew into a rage and swore. The little minister then locked the door, took off his coat and threatened to thrash the factor. This so impressed Peter that he granted the minister a perpetual feu on his chosen site.

Three Young men, 1934. William Charles Young (1851–1934) of Rotha, with his son and partner Robert (1908–57) and Charles Alexander Young, who was killed in France some time later. The firm of solicitors, Grigor & Young, has been served by five generations of Youngs. William Grigor (1804–72), of the Haugh, founded the firm in 1831 with Robert Young (1809–79) of Millbank. Robert's youngest son William Charles Young became a partner. William Gordon Young (1911–78), the founder's great-grandson, worked with the firm from 1946 to 1972 and his great-great-grandson is now a partner in the firm.

The wedding of Dr Thow and Mabel Robertson, after the First World War. When the newly qualified Dr Thow came to Elgin he was assistant to Dr Taylor of Dunfermline House. Some older residents of the town recall the sight of the young Dr Thow, fresh from Aberdeen where he had trained, riding around Elgin on his motor bike while wearing his bowler hat. Mabel was his first wife, who sadly died young.

Jimmy Wood, early 1950s. As well as being a respected local writer, raconteur, naturalist, whisky connoisseur and an amateur artist, Jimmy was an accomplished engineer and enjoyed carrying out repair work on his beloved motor bike. He repaired and restored guns and rifles and also spent many hours creating the most exquisite flies for his other passion of fly fishing.

Jimmy Wood, 1960s. Jimmy was a frequent visitor to Pitgaveny and knew the area and Spynie woods well. Accompanying this photograph that he sent to a friend one Christmas, Jimmy wrote:

> When the last big bottle's empty,
> And the dawn creeps grey and cold,
> When the last clan tartan's folded,
> And the last damned lie's been told,
> Ye'll find them doon in Spynie wood,
> Wi' Zulu – streemin' strang!
> And every time a doo's been missed,
> It's the cartridge that's wrang!

P.S. Doo is about right range for me!

Zulu was the name of one of the special curly-coated retrievers favoured by the Lairdie and used on Pitgaveny estate.

Moray and Nairn Joint County Council. The date is sometime in the 1960s, and there are many well-known faces here. Back row, left to right: William Adam of Glasgreen, Sir William Gordon-Cumming, Dr John Dewar, MO Health, Bill Stephen, Dr John Dean, -?-, George Christie, Dr L. Dean, chairman of the Health Committee, -?-, Alistair Nicol Russell (the ironmonger), David Emslie of Coxton, Lt-Col A.D.

Mackintosh, Andrew Thomson, Deputy County Clerk; -?-, -?-, Mr Barr, Treasurer of Moray and Nairn County Council, William Hutcheson, Sanitary Inspector, -?-. Seated: Neil Robertson of Linkwood, Brig. Grant Peterkin, Capt. James Brander Dunbar, John Petrie, Lt-Col. K. Mackessack, Convenor, Capt. Iain Tennant, John Dean, -?-, Robert McGill, County Clerk and Clerk to the Lieutenancy.

Visit of the Elgin Society to RNAS Lossiemouth, 1968. Included in this photograph are three very prominent members whose efforts over the years contributed so much to the Elgin Society and museum and to local society as a whole. Second from the left is Miss Ethel Rhynas. A well-travelled teacher of disadvantaged children, she was a stalwart supporter of the museum and spent many hours cataloguing in the then unheated building. She began Saturday morning museum activities for children and was at one time president of the Elgin Society (now the Moray Society). On her left is E.S. Harrison, Lord Provost and owner of Johnston's woollen mill, fondly known as 'The Baillie of the Beild'. On the far right is Ernest Thomas, who, under the pen name 'Tuessis' (the Roman name for the Spey), wrote a regular nature column in the *Northern Scot*.

James Brander Dunbar Brander, 1896.
Capt. James Brander Dunbar Brander
(1825–1902) was born Dunbar, and took the
additional name of Brander when his mother
inherited the Brander property of Pitgaveny.
He was a captain of the Scots Greys in the
Crimean War and married Alice Grant,
youngest daughter of James 'Glen' Grant, in
1874. His eldest son James (1875–1969)
eventually became known as 'The Lairdie'.

'Me and my youngest boy.' This photo would
have been taken in the 1890s. Capt. James
Brander Dunbar Brander is clutching his
unmistakable bonnet and standing proudly with
Archibald Alexander Dunbar Brander
(1877–1954). Young Archie served in the
Imperial Forest Service, Central Provinces,
India. He was the author of *Wild Animals of
Central India* and on his retirement lived at Ivy
Bank, Bishopmill.

James Brander Dunbar, 'The Lairdie' (1875–1969). Possibly an official birthday portrait, this shows the young lairdie in typical kilted style with one of his beloved curly-coated retrievers at his feet. The Lairdie was the inspiration for John Buchan's book *John MacNab* (1927). He was captain in the Queen's Own Cameron Highlanders and was active in the Boer War (1899–1902), the First World War, and in the Home Guard in the Second World War. He was very aware of his responsibilities as a major landowner and feudal superior, and as well as his many other interests he took an active involvement in local affairs.

Capt. James Brander Dunbar. The photograph, taken after the Boer War during which Capt. Dunbar saw active service, is dated 6 August 1903. He is wearing his African medals on his Cameron uniform.

The Lairdie and the actor, 1950s. James Robertson Justice on one of his visits to Pitgaveny is examining the Bothgowan stone in the grounds of Pitgaveny House. The name Pitgaveny is an ancient one, probably derived from the Pictish language. The Bothgowan stone supposedly marks the spot where legend says King Duncan was fatally wounded by Macbeth in 1040. To the horror of local antiquaries, the Lairdie dug up the stone to see if there was anything of interest underneath. All he obtained was a large unrewarding hole in his lawn.

Wedding group outside Fife House, Garmouth (now demolished), 9 August 1893. The wedding was of George Geddes and Barbara Marshall Thomson. Everyone is identified. Back row, left to right: John Geddie Spence (Jack) (1873–1953) who was a pilot on the Clyde; Alexander Prendergast Spence (Pren) (1871–1946), who went to Australia; Isabelle Spence (Bette) (1877–1953), who married Hamish Whitelaw; Joseph Duncan, another Clyde pilot, next to his wife, Elizabeth Spence (Lizzie) (1857–1928), daughter of James Spence and Elizabeth Gray; Dr William Geddie, doctor at Accrington, Lancs, next to Margaret Spence (Maggie) (1852–94), daughter of James Spence and Elizabeth Gray; the groom, George Geddes; the bride, Barbara Marshall Thomson Spence (1867–1953); Hugh Thomson Spence (1864–1933), merchant, The Cross, Garmouth; Mary Ann Spence (Polly) (1874–1951); William Hustwick Spence (Willie) (1865–1947), journalist, London; James Spence (Jimmy) (1869–1909), chemist, Elgin. Middle row: James Spence (1828–1901), merchant, The Cross, Garmouth; Mary Ann Hustwick Thomson (Granny Thomson) (1814–1905); Barbara Marshall Thomson Spence (1836–1909). Front row, seated on rugs: Colin Geddie, son of Dr and Mrs Geddie (1884–1955); George Cumming Spence (1879–1950); Burgess Geddie, son of Dr and Mrs Geddie (1887–1957); Jean Cobban Spence (Jeannie) (1882–1950); Jim Geddie and Alan Geddie, sons of Dr and Mrs Geddie.

The Thomson sisters of Corskie, Garmouth, 1885. Standing on the left is Jean (born 1859), who married the headmaster of Balnacoul school, Alex Geddie, son of James Geddie, Speymouth shipbuilder. Standing on the right is Charlotte (born 1866), who married Hugh Spence. Seated on the left is Isabella (born 1862), who married Dr George Geddie, doctor at Garmouth. In the foreground is May (born 1860), who married James Dawson.

Hugh and Charlotte Spence of The Neuk, Garmouth, with their eldest son, James, 1895. As a captain in the Seaforth Highlanders, James was awarded the Military Cross in the First World War. Subsequently he became a lieutenant-colonel in the Indian Rajputana Rifles Regiment and served in India from 1918 until the end of the Second World War. James married Margaret Falconer of Falcon House, Garmouth.

Tommy, the incomer. Elgin became the much-loved adopted home for many people who contributed greatly to the community. Tomasz Zdislaw Kozlowski, born in 1916 in Turek, Poland, was the son of Staislaw Kozlowski, a college director in Poland. Tomasz was educated at the Military Academy until 1935. He joined the Polish Army from 1935 to 1946 and was in the Polish Resettlement Corps, ex-Polish Regiment, and armed forces in France in 1946. He eventually settled, married and raised a family in Elgin. He can be seen on page 68 helping with plans for the D-Day landings.

The end of an era, 1979. Tommy attending the farewell presentation of his friend and colleague at Bilbohall, Geordie Peterkin. From the left: Nancie Robertson, Tommy, Vera Young, George Peterkin, John Young, Mary Bissett, Margaret Allan, Mildred Peterkin, Ian Allan, Mina Murray, Danny Murray. Tommy retired in 1981 and died in 1994, aged seventy-eight.

Tommy's colleagues, 1950s. Tommy took up psychiatric nursing at Elgin's Bilbohall hospital and obtained his qualifications in 1952. He became a great union man and served in the Confederation Of Health Service Employees for many years, much to the benefit of his colleagues. Front row, left to right: House Steward Roddy McLean, Nurse T. Reid, Miss Macdonald, Matron of Bilbohall, psychiatrists Dr Dymock and Dr Gordon, Miss McCabe, Assistant Matron, Nurse Harris, Stanley Forsyth, the minister from Lhanbryde. Second row: -?-, Nurse George, Nurse Donaldson, Rachel Walker, N. Allan, John Brian, Mary Macdonald, -?-, Tom Reid, -?-, N. Stewart, Peter Ellis, Bob McLeod, -?-, 'Birkie' Grant, the farm Grieve (farm bailiff). Third row: Sandy Webster, James Inch, Sandy Fraser, Brian Wier, George Robertson, Davie Mulholland, George Peterkin, ? Mone, Tommy Kozlowski, Ian ?, Bob Rankin, Eric Robertson, John Smith. Back row: Isobel Stables, -?-, Belle Eddie, -?-, -?-, Sheena Cooper, Betty Stacey.

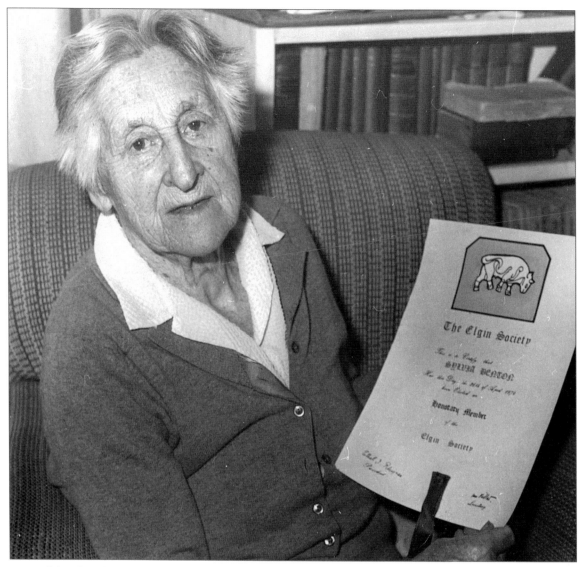

Sylvia Benton MA, DLitt, FSA, FSA Scot, with her certificate of Honorary Membership of the Elgin Society, 1974. Her family was from Speyside although she was born in Lahore, India, in 1887 where her father was a judge. Educated at Girton College, Cambridge, she taught Classics at both Cambridge and Oxford. During a holiday at her father's home in Lossiemouth she began exploring the caves at Covesea and, aged thirty, decided to take up archaeology. Her wish to become one of the first female archaeologists was met with much opposition within the profession, but the famous Gordon Childe, whom she met in Greece in the late 1920s, encouraged her ambitions. Her principal contribution to Scottish archaeology was made between 1928 and 1930 when she carried out excavations at the Sculptor's Cave, Covesea. She retired to Lossiemouth and took a keen interest in the Elgin Society, for a short while becoming the honorary curator of Elgin Museum, and was elected as one of the few Honorary Members of the Elgin Society. She died in 1985 at the age of ninety-eight.

Grandma Wallis, 1934. The granny of wee Jean of Elgin (page 73), this sprightly old lady looks splendid in her fur collar and glorious fancy hat. The photograph was sent as a Christmas greeting and no doubt gave as much pleasure then as it still does now!

Lossiemouth beach, August 1938. Alexander Davidson, seated, then aged eighty, was a train engine driver between Elgin and Aberdeen for nearly fifty years. A native of Insch, he moved to Elgin in 1881. Known as the 'Masher' because of his immaculate appearance, he was said to be 'a rale bull swaggerer o' a man, but aye verra ceevil'. He died shortly after this photograph was taken. Seated beside him is his daughter Ruth, and in front his granddaughter Edith, niece of the footballer Frank Mitchell (page 98). Alexandra Davidson and Connie McGeorge are standing behind.

Duffus House, 1926. On the occasion of their marriage Sir Edward and Lady Dunbar of Northfield were presented with a silver salver by the staff. The unmistakable figure of the Laird of Pitgaveny is fifth from the right. Highfield House, Elgin, was originally Northfield House, the town house of the Dunbars of Northfield. From 1373 to 1429 the family were Constables of the Castle and representatives of the Kings of Scotland in the Province of Moray.

Life on the Gordon estate. It was not all hard work and Francis Vass is taking some convincing about another old fishy tale from Speyside:

'Francis man! You should hae seen the ane I lost – at least five fit lang!'
'Aye aye Geordie, I catched a lantern there yestreen, an it was still lichted.'
'Come on noo Francis, surely that's a lee!'
'Weel Geordie, I'll tell ye fit – tak twa feet aff the fish ye lost an I'll put oot ma licht!'

CHAPTER 10

COUNTRY LIFE

L ife in Elgin city is inextricably interwoven with life in the country. Relatively well sheltered, the Moray coast has more sunshine in the winter months than London. The scarcity of fog was instrumental in the Royal Air Force establishing two important bases in the area. When well clad, Elgin folk are not averse to enjoying the fresh air – there is after all plenty of it around!

A day out at Loch Spynie, 1903. From the left, according to the torn label on the picture, are Mary Adam (whose wedding is pictured on page 84), Mr Dunlop, Amy and George (the last person is unknown). Spynie Loch has long been famous for its bulrushes and records mention the custom of schoolchildren pulling bulrushes there in 1653.

A contented couple, before the First World War. Elgin is surrounded with every variety of pleasant countryside, moorlands, river, mountains and coasts, and these assets are fully appreciated by discerning citizens. No names are recorded; it is just known that this is a local couple relaxing during a quiet moorland walk.

Glen Grant House at the turn of the century. A picturesque group are enjoying their ease under the trees, the conservatory visible behind them. It would have needed a considerable number of servants to maintain such an establishment efficiently. Glen Grant House was built in 1885 and demolished in the 1990s.

Shooting party at the turn of the century. It was often recorded in the local paper at this time that many of the proceeds of a shoot, such as rabbit and birds, were donated to the local hospital. These sportsmen are all set for a day on the moors, but it is not clear just what quarry they are after. Normally ponies would have been used to carry home the deer, but the pointers, spaniels and retrievers would suggest that game birds are about to be shot.

Picnic at Covesea, before the First World War. There is no record of this special day out, which was enjoyed by at least fifty people. Local legend says that one of the caves was used as a store by smugglers for their continental brandy and contraband and that there is a passage leading from another cave to the house of Gordonstoun, half a mile away. The most westerly cave, Helg's Hole, was once often frequented by tinkers and vagrants. The Sculptor's Cave, excavated by Sylvia Benton (page 114), contains carvings dating back to Pictish times and has obviously been used throughout the centuries.

Sunday School picnic at Duffus, 1913. This Sunday School picnic illustrates the good attendance for such events, with more than fifty individuals present in this picture. The original church, now a well-preserved ruin with surrounding ancient graveyard, was known as St Peter's Kirk and stood near Duffus House. The new church at Duffus was built in 1868.

Charlie Scott out on a shoot with his pal Jimmy
'Boy' Wood, 1950s. (Charlie is also pictured
on page 54.) Judging by the rifles they are
carrying their quarry was deer. On one
occasion Jimmy managed to avoid arousing the
suspicion of a gamekeeper after a successful
shoot. With the aid of goggles and scarf, the
deer became the extra passenger in the sidecar
of a motor bike, and so was swiftly removed
from the scene of the kill.

On the moors, at the turn of the century. A lovely day for a shooting party, and among the gun dogs is a
curly-coated retriever, beloved by the Laird of Pitgaveny. Attitudes and times have changed over the
century. Once trophy hunting was perfectly acceptable, and many of the large houses were proud to
display, as part of the decor, large and small game that they had shot or captured either locally or in more
exotic places. Nowadays the wholesale slaughter of the past which wiped out or endangered species is
recognized as no longer defensible.

The Laird of Pitgaveny 1921. Sartorially distinctive as always, Capt. Dunbar is with one of his curly-coated retrievers beside Loch Spynie. Once the loch extended over a large area – in 1779 the loch was 5 miles long with several stepping-stones and ferries. The Spynie canal, designed by Thomas Telford in 1808, was destroyed in the great flood of 1829 and rebuilt in 1860.

A shooting group at Loch Spynie, August 1921. From left to right: Mrs Malcolm Peake, Roger Peake, Capt. Whitaker (seated), Mrs Whitaker, with a then fashionable Pekinese dog, Mr C.W. McAndrew, Col. Hopton, Col. Whitaker sitting on chair. On the far right is 'Ross', the gamekeeper. Sitting on the ground is young Louis Ross who followed in his father's footsteps and became gamekeeper at Pitgaveny.

The Lairdie and friends. Capt. James Brander Dunbar feeds a tame deer while the Pitgaveny keeper, Louis Ross, keeps an eye on the curly-coated retriever and the otter at his feet. Louis and the Lairdie had a special relationship based on their love and knowledge of the wildlife of Pitgaveny and their capacity to speak freely, if not bluntly, to each other.

Loch Spynie, early part of the century. A friend recalled that the Lairdie and Louis Ross, the Pitgaveny keeper, were out fishing on the loch one day when the boat got stuck in the muddy reed beds. The Lairdie told Louis to get out and push and was succinctly told by Louis 'Get oot yoursel' and push. I'm not going to get wet – ye've got a warm fire to go home to'. The Lairdie, seeing the logic in this, duly got out and pushed the boat out of the reeds.

Elsie Fraser with baby Elsie, 1930s. She is wearing a most beautifully knitted cardigan, such fine and fancy work once being the norm. It was usual, where possible, to have hens in the back yard to provide a constant supply of fresh eggs for household cooking and baking and perhaps to earn a little 'pin money' for the housewife.

In a local garden, 1880s. Walled gardens provided shelter for fruit, flowers and vegetables and every big house in the district was well provided for with produce from its own gardens, proudly grown by the team of dedicated gardeners. This group of unnamed folk seem well content in their sunny and sheltered spot. The old lady is wearing a most elaborate lace cap, called a 'mutch', and the costume of the woman standing on the left is a tribute to the strength of whalebone.

Beach huts at Lossiemouth, 1920s. Many folk still talk nostalgically about the family huts on the local beaches. Providing shelter, privacy and storage, they enabled families to spend many happy hours on the coast without having to travel too far from home.

Hugh and Bette at Alves, 1930s. Pre-war days of sunshine and cottages with roses round the door. A grocery shop was at the back of the cottage and the building eventually became the well-known Crook Inn.

ACKNOWLEDGEMENTS

So many people have given generously of their time, information and precious photographs. Not all of them are members of the Moray Society, but on learning that the proceeds were all to go to this local charity, they were only too willing to help. Without their help there would have been no book. Grateful thanks are due to:

Mrs Cathy Adams • Mrs J. Angus • Mrs Barber • Mrs Susan Bennett • Andy Brooks • Mrs Clayton • Alexander Dunbar • Hamish and Ann Dyce • James Dempster • James Falconer • Sammy Fraser • Mrs B. Geddes • Mrs Oonagh Grigor • Mrs G. Haines • Miss I. Henderson • Ian and Kerstin Keillar • S. Kelman • Dr R. Knox • Miss H. Lamont • Mrs F. Macintosh • Mrs E.M. McLean • Mrs Margaret McVey • Moray Golf Club, Lossiemouth • Miss M. Mustard • Mrs I. Paterson • Mrs L. Paterson • George Peterkin • Mrs Ann Ross • Mrs E. Ross • Sinclair Ross • Mrs S. Sammons • Hebbie Smith • Mrs A.D. Spence • Tony Spring • Norman Stewart • Mrs H. Third • K. Williamson • Mrs Margaret Winter • Robbie Young • Stephen Young.

BRITAIN IN OLD PHOTOGRAPHS

The Melton Mowbray Album
The History of the Melton Mowbray Pork Pie
Merton, Morden & Mitcham
Middlesbrough
Around Mildenhall
Milton Keynes
Minehead

The Nadder Valley
Newark
The Norfolk Broads
Norfolk at Work
Lambeth, Kennington & Clapham
North Walsham & District
Northallerton
Around Norwich
Nottingham Yesterday & Today

Oldham
Ormskirk & District
Otley & District
Oxford Yesterday & Today
Oxfordshire at Play
Oxfordshire at School
Oxfordshire Yesterday & Today

Penwith
Penzance & Newlyn
Around Pershore
Peterborough
Around Plymouth
Poole
Portslade
Prestwich

Putney & Roehampton

Redditch & the Needle District
Richmond
Rickmansworth
The River Soar
Around Rotherham
Royal Norfolk Regiment
Rugby & District II
Ruislip
Around Rutland
Around Ryde

Saffron Walden
St Albans
St Andrews
Salford
Salisbury II
Sandhurst & Crowthorne
Sandown & Shanklin
Around Seaton & Sidmouth
Sedgley & District
Sedgley & District II
Sheffield
Sherwood Forest
Shoreham-by-Sea
Lost Shrewsbury
Southampton
Southend-on-Sea
Southwark, Bermondsey & Rotherhithe
Southwark, Bermondsey & Rotherhithe II
Southwell
Stafford

Around Staveley
Stepney, Bethnal Green & Poplar
The History of Stilton Cheese
Stockport
Stoke Newington, Stamford Hill & Upper Clapton
Stourbridge, Wollaston & Amblecote
Stowmarket
Stratford, West Ham & the Royal Docks
Streatham II
Stretford
Stroud & the Five Valleys
Stroud & the Five Valleys II
Suffolk
Suffolk at Work II
Sunderland
Sutton
A Swindon Album
Swindon III

Around Tamworth
Along the Thames
Around Thirsk
Tipton
Tipton II
Around Tonbridge
Torquay
Around Truro
Twickenham, Hampton & Teddington

Uley, Dursley & Cam
Upminster & Hornchurch

The Upper Fal
Uxbridge 1950–1970

Ventnor

Wallingford
Walsall Revisited
Waltham Abbey
Walton-on-Thames & Weybridge
Wandsworth at War
Around Warwick
Weardale
Weardale II
Wednesbury
Wembley & Kingsbury
West Wight
Weymouth & Portland
Around Wheatley
Around Whetstone, Totteridge & Finchley
Whitchurch to Market Drayton
Wigton & the Solway Plain
Willesden
Wimbledon
Around Windsor
Wisbech
Witham & District
The Witney District
Wokingham
The Women's Land Army
Woolwich
Worcestershire at Work
Wordsworth's Lakeland
Wotton-under-Edge to Chipping Sodbury

SUTTON'S PHOTOGRAPHIC HISTORY OF TRANSPORT

Jaguar
Jensen & Jensen-Healey
Lotus
Morgan
Rolls-Royce

TVR
Vauxhall
Suffolk Transport
Manchester Road & Rail
Manchester Ship Canal

Black Country Railways
Cheshire Railways
Derbyshire Railways
Devon Railways
Lancashire Railways

Shropshire Railways
Warwickshire Railways
Worcestershire Railways
Steam around Reading
Steam around Salisbury